COOL RIDES
IN WATER

HYDROPLANES, MINI SUBS AND MORE

by Tyler Omoth

raintree

a Capstone company — publishers for children

Raintree is an imprint of Capstone Global Library Limited, a company incorporated in England and Wales having its registered office at 264 Banbury Road, Oxford, OX2 7DY – Registered company number: 6695582

www.raintree.co.uk
myorders@raintree.co.uk

Edited by Carrie Sheely
Designed by Juliette Peters
Original illustrations © Capstone Global Library Limited 2022
Picture research by Jo Miller
Production by Katy LaVigne
Originated by Capstone Global Library Ltd
Printed and bound in India

978 1 3982 0343 3 (hardback)
978 1 3982 0344 0 (paperback)

British Library Cataloguing in Publication Data
A full catalogue record for this book is available from the British Library.

Acknowledgements
We would like to thank the following for permission to reproduce photographs: Alamy: CTK, 11, Keystone Press, 19; AP Images: Ted S. Warren, 18; Getty Images: Icon Sports Wire/Contributor, 17, Wild Horizon/Contributor, 21; Newscom: Cover Images/Migaloo Submarines, 28, SIPA/UNIMEDIA-US, 5, ZUMA Press/Caters News, 29, ZUMA Press/Innespace, 27, ZUMA Press/Ralph Lauer, 10; Shutterstock: De Visu, 6, DO-P, 12, Marcel Jancovic, 15, R_Pilguj, 7, Sebw, 22, sergios, 4, Sheila Fitzgerald, 9, Stephen Clarke, Cover, tridland, 8; U.S. Navy, 25, U.S. Navy photo by Mass Communication Specialist 1st Class Daniel Barker, 13, Mass Communication Specialist 2nd Class Christopher A. Veloicaza, 23.
Design elements: Capstone; Shutterstock: teerayut tae

CONTENTS

Words in **bold** are in the glossary.

Awesome technology in the water

A speedboat zips across a lake. Water sprays behind the boat as it skips across the water. People have been travelling in boats for thousands of years. Today, **technology** has come a long way. The advanced vehicles you see on the water are proof. Some transport cargo and do other jobs, but some are just for fun.

Modern speedboats reach speeds of more than 161 kilometres (100 miles) per hour.

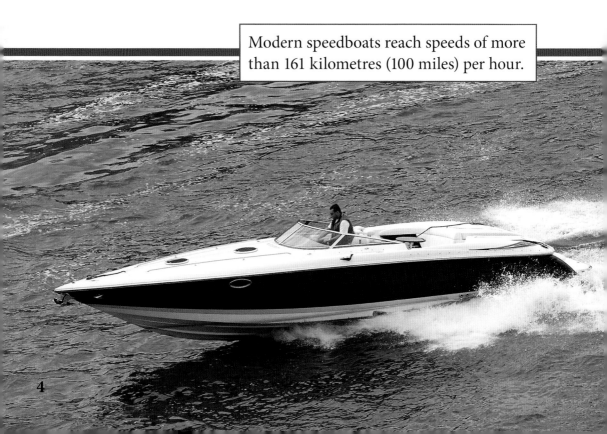

The Seabreacher travels both underwater and on the water's surface with ease.

Water vehicles come in many shapes and sizes. People can hover just above the water in a small hovercraft or dip below the waves in mini submarines. Some watercraft can even travel both underwater and above water. Discover some of the coolest water vehicles around!

Yachts

Yachts are boats that come in many different sizes. Most are more than 12 metres (40 feet) long. But some of the largest yachts can measure more than 152 m (500 feet) long!

Yachts have many uses. Whether people want to use them for fishing, racing or just relaxing, there is a yacht that will be a perfect fit. Some people race sailing yachts long distances in oceans. These boats have sails that catch the wind to move them along.

In the correct weather conditions, sailing yachts need only wind to move them.

Many yachts are large and built for **luxury**. They have many rooms and much more than just space for eating and sleeping. They may have swimming pools or even basketball courts on board! Many people can travel on one of these yachts at once. They can be very expensive to own.

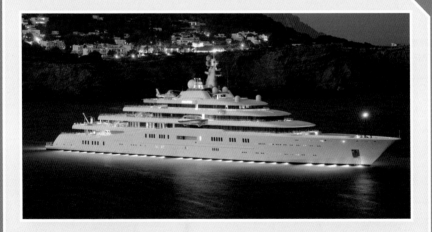

The *Eclipse*

One of the most expensive yachts in the world is called the *Eclipse*. It has nine decks on it. There are helicopter pads, swimming pools, a car garage and even a dance floor. It's the ultimate fun boat. The *Eclipse* is valued at a whopping £1 billion.

Tugboats

Have you ever seen a little boat pushing a much bigger boat? Those mighty little boats are called tugboats. Tugboats may not be very big, but they are powerful.

It can be very hard for large ships to steer safely into ports. Tugboats push or pull the larger boats. They safely steer them to where they need to go.

A tugboat pulls a ship through the Corinth Canal in Greece.

Many tugboats work together to steer a big cargo ship into a port in California, USA.

To move the big ships, tugboats need very powerful engines. Their engines are like the ones that run heavy trains on land. The average tugboat engine makes 680 to 3,400 **horsepower**. Most cars have less than 200 horsepower.

Some tugboats are built to do jobs besides moving larger boats. Some have firefighting equipment. They can pump water from the lake or ocean that they are sailing on to put out fires. Other tugboats have equipment on the front to help them break up ice.

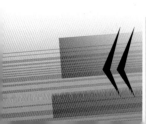

FACT

People around the world hold tugboat races.

Foilboards

Can you imagine riding a surfboard away from the waves near the coast and out into the open water? With foilboards, you can!

Foilboards are surfboards that use a hydrofoil. A hydrofoil is a long fin attached to the surfboard's bottom. It lifts the board out of the water as it travels. Some foilboards have a motor. These boards can move up to 40 km (25 miles) per hour on the water.

For extra fun, some people use a kite to help pull their boards through the water. This is called kiteboarding. When kiteboarding with a hydrofoil, the rider can get a very fast, smooth ride.

A man rides a kiteboard with a hydrofoil in a river.

A man rides an electric foilboard in the Czech Republic.

Discovering early surfers

In 1778, explorer James Cook landed in Hawaii with his crew. His crew members recorded seeing people riding long, flat pieces of wood out in the water. They noted that a surfer who made it to the shore before falling off would be praised by his friends. These were some of the earliest known surfers.

Hovercraft

Imagine being out on a boat racing towards the shoreline. When you get to land, your boat keeps going right up the beach and onto land! With a hovercraft, you can travel across water and land. It's the ultimate **amphibious** vehicle.

A hovercraft uses a fan to blast air beneath it. This forms a cushion of air that allows the vehicle to hover above the surface. Another fan pushes the hovercraft forward by blowing air behind the vehicle.

A hovercraft in the UK carries passengers between Ryde and Southsea.

Hovercraft have many uses. The US military uses them to move troops and equipment from ships to shores. Large hovercraft are used as ferry boats in some places. Ferry boats carry people and cars from one side of a body of water to the other.

FACT:

The US military uses a hovercraft called the Landing Craft Air Cushion (LCAC). The large hovercraft can carry 75 tonnes of cargo. It is so big it can even haul a tank!

People use small hovercrafts for fun. Some places rent them out for people to ride. There are even hovercraft golf carts!

Some people race hovercraft in organized events. The racecourses often include both land and water. The Hoverclub of America organizes several types of races. Classes are based on the age of the racer as well as the hovercraft's engine and other parts. Racers complete a series of laps around a course.

Top racers compete in the World Hovercraft Championships. Bob Windt broke the hovercraft speed record at the 1995 World Championships. He went 137.4 km (85.38 miles) per hour.

A hovercraft racer speeds through a course in Slovakia.

Hydroplanes

A bright hydroplane streaks across the water. A huge stream of water rises into the air behind it. Its engine makes a roaring sound like thunder. Another hydroplane is screaming along right behind it. Both racers are fighting to cross the finish line first.

Hydroplanes are built for speed. They can reach top speeds of more than 400 km (250 miles) per hour. Their **aerodynamic** bodies easily cut through the air. Their bodies are made of a variety of lightweight materials, including carbon fibre and aluminium. A large cover over the engine called a cowling sits behind the **cockpit**. It draws air into the engine to help it produce more power.

The huge sprays of water that shoot out from behind hydroplanes are called rooster tails.

Hydroplanes compete in an H1 Unlimited series race in Seattle, Washington, USA.

A hydroplane barely touches the water. At high speeds, the front of the boat lifts out of the water. The boat then skims over the water. This helps the boat go faster. There is little **friction** between the boat and the water to slow it down.

Many hydroplanes use jet engines. These large, loud engines give hydroplanes their nickname of "thunderboats".

Racing at such high speeds can be dangerous. Hydroplanes are designed to keep drivers safe. The cockpit is completely enclosed. In the case of an accident, it is designed to stay together even if the rest of the boat is destroyed.

 FACT:
The hydroplane speed record belongs to Australian Ken Warby. He zoomed to 511.095 km (317.58 miles) per hour.

Mini subs

Have you ever dreamed of exploring the deepest parts of the oceans? Today, miniature submarines, or mini subs, make it possible. Sometimes these vehicles are called submersibles. Most mini subs are designed to carry one or two people.

People design mini subs for different uses. Militaries sometimes use them to help crews make sneak attacks near enemy coasts. Some mini subs are designed for fun. The Triton Submarines company designed a recreational mini sub that can travel 2,286 m (7,500 feet) underwater. Other mini subs are designed for research. Much of the ocean's deepest parts are unexplored. Scientists want to know what plants and sea animals are there. Some research subs have advanced cameras and equipment to gather samples of what is found.

People in a mini sub get an up-close look at a sponge on a coral reef.

Catamarans

You're racing along the water on a catamaran. The wind catches in the sail, pushing you faster and faster. Finally, you inch ahead of the catamaran in front of you as you head to the finish line.

Catamaran boats have two **hulls** that are connected in the middle. They come in many sizes and types. Some have sails, while motors power others. Some people race sailing catamarans that have hydrofoils. The hydrofoils push the boats out of the water to help them go faster. Top teams from around the world race in the famous America's Cup.

Catamaran racers compete in Sweden.

The USNS *Spearhead* (front) and the other EPFs have hulls made of aluminium.

Militaries also use catamarans. The US Navy uses catamarans as high-speed transport vehicles. They are called Expeditionary Fast Transports (EPFs). They can travel at 64 km (40 miles) per hour. They can carry 600 tonnes of cargo.

Guided missile destroyers

The US Navy's guided missile destroyers are very large warships. The newest class of guided missile destroyers are in the Zumwalt class. These ships are 186 m (610 feet) long. They are designed to be hard for enemy **radar** to detect. This helps the boats more easily sneak into enemy territory. The destroyers can defend against enemy submarines, ships and aircraft.

One hundred and seventy-five crew members operate a Zumwalt-class destroyer. That may seem like a lot, but other similar ships need nearly twice as many crew members. New technology allows many of the ship's functions to be fully **automated**. One ship costs about £5.7 billion to build.

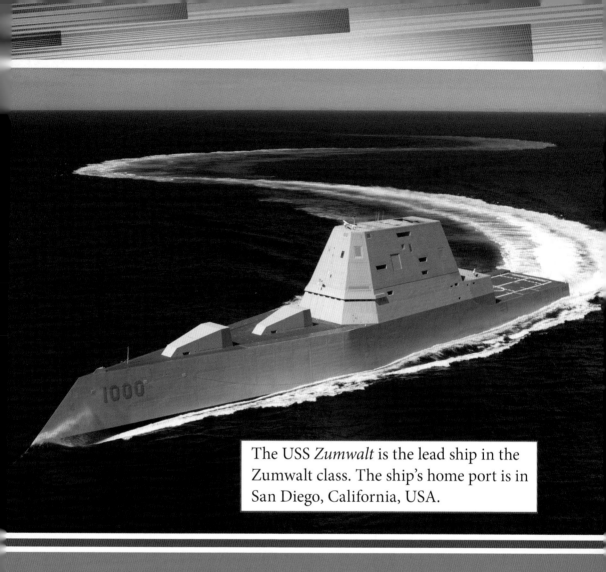

The USS *Zumwalt* is the lead ship in the Zumwalt class. The ship's home port is in San Diego, California, USA.

What's in a name?

Each ship in the US Navy has a name. How it is named is based on what type of ship it is. For example, guided missile cruisers are named after important Americans or famous battles. In the British Royal Navy, ships are often named after royalty. 'HMS' before a ship's name stands for 'Her (or His) Majesty's Ship'.

Seabreachers

Imagine you're racing along the water at 80 km (50 miles) per hour in a boat. What if that same boat could dive below the surface like a mini sub? A Seabreacher can do both!

The Seabreacher is shaped like a large shark with a top fin. This super-fun vehicle can race along the top of the water or dive 1.5 m (5 feet) beneath the waves. It can also roll over. It can even dive down and then **breach** the surface like a shark can! Some are even painted to look like sharks.

A camera is mounted on the nose of the sub. The camera lets the riders take video of their adventures above and below the water's surface.

The Seabreacher can travel up to 3.7 m (12 feet) in the air.

The future of cool rides in water

Watercraft have come a long way. They've gone from simple boats used for fishing and crossing rivers to speedy hydroplanes and huge yachts.

Designers will continue to find ways to advance watercraft technology. They will try to make them go faster and ride more smoothly. In the future, more watercraft may run on electricity instead of by burning fuels. These electric watercraft will be better for the **environment**. A company called SeaBubbles designed an electric boat called the Bubble Taxi. It lifts up on hydrofoils as its speed increases.

Submersible yachts are one idea that designers have for the future.

A Chinese inventor created the Volkswagen
Aqua concept for a car design competition.
It works like a hovercraft.

There may even be completely new watercraft
designs in the future. Some designers have created
concepts to show how their ideas for new watercraft
might work. If you could design a new watercraft,
what would you make?

GLOSSARY

aerodynamic ability of something to move easily and quickly through the air

amphibious able to work on land or water

automate run automatically by mechanical or electronic devices

breach jump out of the water

cockpit place where a driver sits in certain types of vehicle

concept idea for a new way to build or create something

environment air, water, trees and other natural surroundings

friction force produced when two objects rub against each other; friction slows down objects

horsepower unit for measuring an engine's power

hull main body of a boat

luxury something that you do not really need but that is enjoyable to have

radar device that uses radio waves to track the location of objects

technology use of science to do practical things, such as designing complex machines

FIND OUT MORE

BOOKS

Cars, Trains, Ships and Planes: A Visual Encyclopedia of Every Vechicle, DK (DK Children, 2015)

The History of Transport (The History of Technology), Chris Oxlade (Raintree, 2017)

Motion Projects to Build On (STEM Projects), Marne Ventura (Raintree, 2020)

WEBSITES

www.bbc.co.uk/bitesize/topics/zc89k7h/articles/zytqj6f
Learn about buoyancy.

www.dkfindout.com/uk/transport
Find out more about different types of transport.

INDEX